LEADERS OF WORLD WAR II

BY YVETTE LaPIERRE

CONTENT CONSULTANT
Brett L. Walker
Regents Professor of History
Montana State University, Bozeman

Cover image: British military leaders posed with Prime Minister
Winston Churchill, *center*, on May 7, 1945.

Core Library

An Imprint of Abdo Publishing
abdobooks.com

abdobooks.com

Published by Abdo Publishing, a division of ABDO, PO Box 398166, Minneapolis, Minnesota 55439. Copyright © 2025 by Abdo Consulting Group, Inc. International copyrights reserved in all countries. No part of this book may be reproduced in any form without written permission from the publisher. Core Library™ is a trademark and logo of Abdo Publishing.

Printed in the United States of America, North Mankato, Minnesota.
052024
092024

Cover Photo: Paul Popper/Popperfoto/Getty Images
Interior Photos: Album/Alamy, 4–5; Daily Herald Archive/National Science & Media Museum/SSPL/Getty Images, 6, 43; Red Line Editorial, 8, 38; Bettmann/Getty Images, 10; David J. & Janice L. Frent/The Front Collection/Corbis Premium Historical/Getty Images, 12; Heinrich Hoffmann/adoc-photos/Corbis Historical/Getty Images, 14–15; Hudson/Topical Press Agency/Hulton Archive/Getty Images, 19; Fox Photos/Hulton Archive/Getty Images, 21; Popperfoto/Getty Images, 24; Wikimedia Commons, 26–27; Icon and Image/Michael Ochs Archives/Getty Images, 32–33, 45; PhotoQuest/Archive Images/Getty Images, 37; Universal History Archive/Universal Images Group/Getty Images, 39

Editor: Marley Richmond
Series Designer: Ryan Gale

Library of Congress Control Number: 2023949171

Publisher's Cataloging-in-Publication Data

Names: LaPierre, Yvette, author.
Title: Leaders of world war II / by Yvette LaPierre
Description: Minneapolis, Minnesota: Abdo Publishing, 2025 | Series: World war II | Includes online resources and index.
Identifiers: ISBN 9781098293659 (lib. bdg.) | ISBN 9798384912927 (ebook)
Subjects: LCSH: World War, 1939-1945--Juvenile literature. | Heads of state--Juvenile literature. | Leadership--Juvenile literature. | Armed forces--Juvenile literature. | United States--Juvenile literature. | Politics and government--Juvenile literature.
Classification: DDC 940.53--dc23

CONTENTS

THE TEHRAN CONFERENCE

On November 28, 1943, US president Franklin D. Roosevelt and British prime minister Winston Churchill met with Soviet premier Joseph Stalin for the first time. They were the leaders of the major countries making up the Allied powers. They were in Tehran, Iran, to discuss strategies for a victory in World War II (1939–1945).

The meeting was uneasy at times. Roosevelt and Churchill had been allies and friends for a long time. But Stalin was not

Aleksandr Mikhailovich Gerasimov painted *The Tehran Conference*, which shows a discussion between Allied leaders.

Joseph Stalin, *left*, Franklin D. Roosevelt, *center*, and Winston Churchill, *right*, did not have an easy relationship. But they worked together to make important plans at Tehran.

a traditional ally of the United States and Great Britain. The United States and Britain were opposed to Stalin's Communist government. Stalin was generally pleasant during the conference, though the dictator was difficult at times.

The three leaders ended the conference on December 1. Despite their political differences, they had agreed on many points. Most importantly, they had a plan to cooperate and win the war for the Allied powers.

THE BIG THREE

World War II began on September 1, 1939, when Germany invaded Poland. Before this advancement, tensions had been rising across Europe and separately in the Pacific. Adolf Hitler led Germany's Nazi Party, which had begun working to expand Germany's territory and influence across Europe. The Nazis were nationalist

INVASION OF POLAND

In 1939 Germany and the Soviet Union signed an agreement to invade Poland together. However, Germany turned against the Soviet Union in 1941. The map above shows when German and Soviet troops entered Poland. How does this map help you understand the invasion and Poland's surrender?

and anti-Semitic. Germany's invasion of Poland was an early step toward the Nazi's goal of creating a German empire.

On September 3, Great Britain and France declared war on Germany. These nations became two of the chief Allied nations, eventually joined by the United

States, China, and the Soviet Union. France fought with the Allies until it was occupied by Germany in 1940. The United States joined the war in 1941 after being attacked by Japan. Churchill, Roosevelt, and Stalin became known as the Big Three of the Allied leaders.

The Allies fought against the Axis powers. Germany formed the Axis alliance with Italy and Japan. Benito Mussolini led Italy.

PERSPECTIVES

SPREADING DEMOCRACY

For many Allied nations, fighting in World War II was a matter of national defense. This was especially true for Great Britain, which German troops planned to invade. But in many ways, World War II was also about maintaining and promoting democracy. Democracies defend the right for all citizens to participate in government. Many Axis nations were run by dictators. In a dictatorship, the government is run by one person with absolute power. Individuals rely on the leader to make the best choices for the nation. Defeating dictatorial governments would allow the Allies to promote more democratic systems.

Emperor Hirohito, surrounded by powerful military advisors including Prime Minister Tōjō Hideki, led Japan. All three leaders wanted to gain more power and land. They took extreme, violent actions, and Hitler began a genocide against Jewish people.

WARTIME LEADERS

By its end in 1945, World War II had spread across the globe. It was fought in both Europe and the Pacific. The war affected millions of people, including both the armed forces and civilians. Their fate and the course of the war were in the hands of a small number of leaders.

Political leaders had to make difficult decisions. Their actions could protect people, cities, and economies or put them at risk. They had to know when to share plans with allies and when to keep secrets. Leaders in democratic countries needed to build public support for a deadly and expensive war.

One important Soviet military leader was Georgy Zhukov. He led the Soviet Army to success toward the end of World War II.

Posters celebrated World War II leaders, including Roosevelt, *left*, and Churchill, *right*.

Military leaders commanded the biggest armies, navies, and air forces that the world had ever seen. They planned military strategies, usually while following the orders of their nation's political leaders. Military leaders also tried to guess the plans of their enemies. They had to supply their troops with enough weapons, gear, and food. They had to lift the spirits of their troops.

The leaders shaped the course of the war and of the world to come. The war, in turn, shaped the leaders. Some were set on a path to becoming heroes. For others, the war was the end of their dreams and goals.

STRAIGHT TO THE
SOURCE

Roosevelt, Churchill, and Stalin released a joint declaration following the Tehran Conference. It said:

> *We express our determination that our nations shall work together in war and in the peace that will follow.*
>
> *As to war—our military staffs have joined in our round-table discussions, and we have [coordinated] our plans for the destruction of the German forces. We have reached complete agreement as to the scope and timing of the operations to be undertaken from the east, west, and south.*
>
> *The common understanding which we have here reached guarantees that victory will be ours.*

Source: "December 1, 1943: The Tehran Declaration." *University of Virginia Miller Center*, n.d., millercenter.org. Accessed 19 Oct. 2023.

WHAT'S THE BIG IDEA?

Read this passage carefully. What is the main idea expressed by the three leaders? What details support the main idea?

LEADERS IN EUROPE

After Germany invaded Poland in 1939, Hitler's army marched west. German forces occupied France in 1940. When it became clear that France would fall, Italy joined the war on Germany's side.

In 1941 Germany invaded the Soviet Union. This went against a pact Hitler had signed with Stalin in 1939. The countries had agreed not to fight one another. Once the pact was broken, Stalin joined the Allied powers as war spread throughout Europe. Allied leaders in Europe worked to block Hitler's advances

Adolf Hitler, *center*, posed beside German artists after the German military succeeded in occupying France.

15

during this period. The Soviet Union supplied soldiers, and the United States supplied guns, equipment, and ammunition.

ALLIED LEADERS

Winston Churchill (1874–1965) was a British politician. As early as 1929, he began warning of the danger of the growing Nazi Party in Germany. In 1940 Churchill was elected British prime minister. He proved to be an inspirational leader throughout the war. He was known for wanting to lead by experiencing the action firsthand. In 1944 the king had to prevent Churchill from joining the landing of Allied troops in Normandy, France, known as D-Day.

Churchill was also known and loved by many for his good humor, "V for Victory" hand sign, and stirring speeches. At the beginning of the war, British defeat looked certain. But Churchill led his country to ultimate victory over the Axis powers.

Joseph Stalin (1878–1953) was an unlikely Allied leader. In 1922 Stalin became a leader in the Communist Party of the Soviet Union. He later made himself supreme commander. This put him in charge of major military decisions for his government. Stalin had anyone who might challenge him removed from the government. The Soviet secret police arrested and executed thousands of Stalin's political rivals, and millions of people were sent to prison camps.

Stalin ruled the Soviet Union for more than 20 years. The Communist dictator turned the Soviet

Union into a major world power. He appealed to his citizens to "scorch the earth" ahead of any enemy invasion. Soviets would destroy their own food and factories so invading enemies could not use them. After the war, Stalin turned against the United States and his other World War II allies.

OCCUPIED FRANCE

French leaders were in a difficult position when Germany invaded their country in May 1940. The vice premier was Philippe Pétain (1856–1951), a French general. As German troops poured into France and reached Paris, Pétain began to collaborate with the Nazis. On June 17, he broadcast a message to all French forces to stop fighting. British forces were in France to help fight the Nazis, and the French military abandoned them. After France surrendered, Germany allowed Pétain to govern the southern part of France that remained unoccupied. This area and its government were called Vichy France.

The French general and statesman Charles de Gaulle (1890–1970) was strongly opposed to France's cooperation with Germany. De Gaulle had served in the French Army during World War I. When France surrendered to Germany in 1940, de Gaulle escaped to Britain. He led the Free French forces, who were part of a movement to resist German occupation and the Vichy government. De Gaulle marched with the Allied troops when they liberated France in August 1944.

After France was liberated, Pétain was brought to trial in France for betraying his country. He was found guilty in 1945. He lived the remainder of his life in prison. De Gaulle took office as president of France in 1959.

BENITO MUSSOLINI

Benito Mussolini (1883–1945) founded Italy's Fascist Party and ruled the country as a dictator. He led his country into war on the side of Hitler in the hopes of sharing in Germany's military success. But the Italian Army suffered many defeats, and Italian citizens grew tired of the war.

In July 1943, the Allies began an invasion of Italy. Weeks later, Mussolini's own Fascist Party arrested him. Germans quickly helped him escape. In 1945 he was recaptured by Italians and then shot and killed.

ADOLF HITLER

Adolf Hitler (1889–1945) fought in World War I. He joined the Nazi Party in 1919. After being inspired by Mussolini's Fascist Italy, Hitler rose to power and began ruling Germany as a dictator. He took the title of führer,

Hitler, *right*, first met Mussolini, *left*, in 1934. The leaders met many times over the course of the war.

or leader, in 1934. He wanted to create an empire in Europe made up of what he considered to be a pure German race. To do this, he planned to exterminate Jewish people and others he considered undesirable. His anti-Semitic beliefs led to the Holocaust, during which Nazis killed 6 million Jewish people. Hitler gave rousing speeches to rally supporters and took charge of the military to accomplish his goals.

When Germany started losing, Hitler hid away in a bunker in Berlin and refused to surrender. As Soviet troops entered Berlin, he appointed Admiral Karl Dönitz as his successor. Hitler and his new wife, Eva Braun, died by suicide on April 30, 1945.

NAZI MILITARY

Hitler built a strong army commanded by loyal military leaders. Erwin Rommel (1891–1944) was one of Hitler's early supporters. Rommel was a daring and well-respected commander. During World War II, he earned the nickname "the Desert Fox" during successful battles for control of North Africa. Hitler put Rommel in charge of defending occupied France from the Allied invasion in the summer of 1944. But Rommel failed to stop the D-Day landing, which was a significant turning point in favor of the Allied forces. Rommel grew to dislike Hitler's choices and leadership. Later in 1944, Rommel was accused of participating in a plot to kill Hitler and was arrested. He took poison to end his own life rather than be executed.

Heinrich Himmler (1900–1945) was a military commander and one of the most powerful men in Nazi Germany. Himmler organized and controlled the concentration camps where Jewish people and other enemies of the Nazis were imprisoned and forced into hard labor. He also ordered and oversaw the torture and massacre of millions of men, women, and children in Nazi camps. As the war neared its end, Hitler feared that Himmler was negotiating with the Allies to replace him. Hitler ordered Himmler's arrest. Himmler was captured by British troops on May 23, 1945. He took poison and died before he could be brought to trial.

Hermann Göring (1893–1946) was one of Hitler's close advisors. Göring was the commander of the German Air Force during World War II. His air force was ultimately not successful, and the Allies had command of the air by 1944. Hitler lost faith in Göring, but Göring stayed loyal to the end. He was convicted of war crimes in 1946, but he died by suicide, taking poison before he could be executed.

FURTHER EVIDENCE

Chapter Two briefly covers Hitler and the role of the Nazi Party in World War II. What is one of the chapter's main points about Nazi Germany? What evidence supports this point? Go to the website below. Does it present new evidence?

HOW DID ADOLF HITLER HAPPEN?

abdocorelibrary.com/leaders-world-war-ii

Hermann Göring, *left*, and Heinrich Himmler, *right*, were important Nazi leaders even before World War II began. At times they worked together closely.

LEADERS IN ASIA

While World War II raged in Europe, tensions increased in the Pacific. Like Germany and Italy, Japan was committed to expanding its empire. Japan had been at war with China since 1937. Japan escalated its aggression in the Pacific by invading another Pacific nation in 1940. Weeks later, the empire formed an alliance with Germany and Italy. Japan became a major Axis power. China joined the Allies in 1941.

The United States protested Japanese aggression in China. In an attempt to stop

Chinese leader Chiang Kai-shek led the Chinese military's efforts in support of the Allies.

further Japanese expansion, the US government banned exports of oil to Japan. But Japan still needed oil, and Japanese military leaders knew the United States would interfere if Japan invaded more territories to get it.

On December 7, 1941, the Japanese military bombed the US naval base at Pearl Harbor. Japanese officials believed the attack would distract the United States while Japan advanced elsewhere. The United States joined World War II the next day.

CHINA

Chiang Kai-shek (1887–1975) became leader of the Chinese Nationalist Party in 1925. Two years later, he led a fight against the growing power of the Chinese Communists. The Communists were led by Mao Zedong. Mao and Chiang continued to fight one another while also resisting Japan's attacks. They never successfully worked together to fight Japan, and this left China vulnerable to Japanese forces.

The Allies provided aid and support to Chiang's defiance of Japan. China declared war against Germany, Italy, and Japan in 1941, and Chiang joined the ranks of the top Allied leaders. After the war, in 1949, Chiang's party lost to Mao's Communist Party. Mao led the People's Republic of China, and Chiang was exiled to Taiwan.

JAPAN

Hirohito (1901–1989) became the emperor of Japan in 1926 after the death of his father. Historians debate how

JAPANESE MONARCHY

The role of emperor changed during Hirohito's time in power. For much of history, Japan's emperors rarely participated in politics. Instead the emperor had a divine or ceremonial role. After World War II, the emperor had even less power. Japan adopted a new constitution that gave power to the Japanese citizens. Hirohito's role as emperor became that of symbolizing Japanese unity. He did not have any real political power.

much power Hirohito had over Japan and the Japanese military. Some historians believe he relied on his advisors to make decisions. Others think he was actively involved in Japan's efforts to expand its empire.

However, Hirohito's power over Japan was critical in August 1945, when the United States dropped atomic bombs on two Japanese cities. Hirohito knew that Japan would be destroyed if the country did not surrender. On August 15, Hirohito announced Japan's surrender by radio. After the war, Hirohito continued to serve as emperor until his death in 1989.

One of the advisors Hirohito relied on most was Tōjō Hideki (1884–1948). Tōjō became Japan's vice minister of war in 1938 and served as prime minister from 1941 to 1944. He was a main advocate for joining the Axis powers. Tōjō led Japan's war efforts after the attack on Pearl Harbor.

Tōjō shot himself after Japan surrendered, but he survived. On April 29, 1946, he was found guilty of war crimes and hanged. Many other Japanese wartime leaders were also tried and found guilty.

EXPLORE ONLINE

Chapter Three focuses on the leaders of the main Asian countries involved in World War II. Chiang Kai-shek led China through internal conflicts and World War II. The article at the website below goes into more depth on this topic. Does the article answer any of the questions you had about Chiang?

CHIANG KAI-SHEK

abdocorelibrary.com/leaders-world-war-ii

MBS
NBC
CBS
MBS
CBS
NBC

LEADERS IN THE UNITED STATES

When Churchill declared war on Germany in 1939, the United States supported Great Britain but did not enter the war. The US public was against fighting another war in Europe after World War I. That sentiment quickly changed, however, when Japan bombed Pearl Harbor. The US Congress quickly declared war on Japan. Days later, Germany and Italy declared war on the United States. US political and military leaders soon became an important part of the Allied war efforts.

On December 9, 1941, President Franklin D. Roosevelt spoke over the radio. He addressed the decision to enter World War II.

FRANKLIN D. ROOSEVELT

Franklin D. Roosevelt (1882–1945) became president of the United States in 1933. He was in his third term as president when Japan attacked Pearl Harbor. Roosevelt led the nation through most of World War II.

Under his direction, the United States developed the world's largest and most powerful navy. Roosevelt helped build a massive air force and army. During his presidency, more than 14 million people were drafted into various branches of the military. Roosevelt traveled overseas to plan military strategies

PERSPECTIVES

CODE NAME ROVER

First Lady Eleanor Roosevelt inspired Americans with her efforts in the war. She toured the United States and overseas to boost the morale of soldiers and civilians. Her travels sometimes took her into dangerous war zones. To keep her safe, her security team never mentioned her by name. The security officers called her by the code name Rover. After seeing the horrors of war firsthand, Eleanor Roosevelt was determined to help create lasting world peace.

with other Allied leaders. At home, he gave radio talks to help boost the morale of citizens on the home front.

Roosevelt died suddenly on April 12, 1945, just before the end of the war. Many people at home and abroad considered him an energetic and inspiring leader. Americans and Allies throughout Europe mourned his death.

HARRY S. TRUMAN

Harry S. Truman (1884–1972) served in World War I. He was elected Roosevelt's vice president in 1944, for Roosevelt's fourth term. Truman took the oath of office and became president two hours after Roosevelt's death.

Truman helped arrange Germany's surrender on May 8, 1945. He still had many decisions to make as the war with Japan continued. The most difficult and controversial was his decision to drop atomic bombs on two cities in Japan. The US Army Air Forces dropped an atomic bomb on Hiroshima on August 6, 1945, and another on Nagasaki on August 9. These bombings killed approximately 210,000 people, and they injured many more. Japan surrendered days later.

Truman served as president until 1953. His government helped rebuild cities in Europe devastated by the war. He also oversaw the creation of the United Nations in 1945.

THE UNITED NATIONS

At the end of World War II, the world's leaders and citizens were eager for peace and security. Leaders from 50 nations gathered in April 1945. Two months later, they had drafted a charter to create an international organization dedicated to preventing another world war. Great Britain, China, France, the Soviet Union, the United States, and many other countries signed the charter to form the United Nations.

AMERICAN GENERALS

Dwight D. Eisenhower (1890–1969) and Douglas MacArthur (1880–1964) were two of the most well-known US generals who helped lead the Allies to victory. Eisenhower served in the US military

President Harry S. Truman, *right*, stood beside General Dwight D. Eisenhower, *left*, and General George S. Patton, *center*, at a flag-raising ceremony in 1945. Patton was an important officer in the US Army during World War II.

beginning in 1915. He was a master of war strategy and logistics. He also had a calm and friendly presence that was appreciated by his fellow Allied military leaders.

Eisenhower was the supreme commander of the troops invading Normandy, France, on June 6, 1944. Eisenhower coordinated thousands of Allied troops, ships, and planes in the D-Day invasion. By July about 1 million Allied troops were moving through occupied France. Eisenhower's strategy pushed German troops back to the German border by the end of 1944. The war in Europe was soon over. Eisenhower was a popular war

PREWAR AND POSTWAR
LEADERS

The table below shows how leadership stayed the same for some countries and changed for others during and after World War II. Why might some countries have changed leaders? How does this table help you understand the lasting impacts of World War II?

COUNTRY	PREWAR LEADER	POSTWAR LEADER
Great Britain	**Winston Churchill**, prime minister	**Clement Attlee**, prime minister
China	**Chiang Kai-shek**, head of the Chinese Nationalist Party	**Mao Zedong**, head of the People's Republic of China
France	**Philippe Pétain**, chief of state	**Charles de Gaulle**, head of the provisional government
Germany	**Adolf Hitler**, führer	**France, Great Britain, and the United States**, occupied West Germany; **Soviet Union**, occupied East Germany
Italy	**Benito Mussolini**, prime minister; and **Pietro Badoglio**, prime minister	**Ferruccio Parri**, prime minister
Japan	**Hirohito**, emperor	**Hirohito**, emperor
Soviet Union	**Joseph Stalin**, premier	**Joseph Stalin**, premier
United States	**Franklin D. Roosevelt**, president	**Harry S. Truman**, president

Douglas MacArthur signed the surrender of Japan in a ceremony on September 2, 1945, on behalf of the Allies.

hero who went on to serve as the US president from 1953 to 1961.

General Douglas MacArthur served in both World War I and World War II. He led Allied forces in battles in the Pacific. He was promoted to commander of all US Army forces in the Pacific in 1945. He used an island-hopping strategy to move his troops from island to island. At each stop, he disrupted the supply and communication lines of Japanese troops. This strategy left Axis troops isolated and helped the Allies succeed.

THE WAR ENDS

The war was over in Europe by May 1945. Japan's official surrender on September 2 brought an end to World War II. For six years, battles had raged across Europe and the Pacific, leaving lives and countries in ruins. As a result, the borders of some nations were redrawn, and leadership changed.

Some alliances between the leaders of countries remained intact, such as between Great Britain and the United States. Others shifted. The Soviet Union and the United States emerged as major world powers after the war. But they quickly went from allies to enemies. Roosevelt had hoped that China would become an Asian democracy. But instead, China became a Communist country under the leadership of Mao. The new leaders and alliances between nations would lead the world into the postwar era.

STRAIGHT TO THE
SOURCE

On December 9, 1941, two days after Japan bombed Pearl Harbor, President Roosevelt delivered a radio speech to prepare and motivate Americans for war. He said:

> *We are now in the midst of a war, not for conquest, not for vengeance, but for a world in which this nation, and all that this nation represents, will be safe for our children. We expect to eliminate the danger from Japan, but it would serve us ill if we accomplished that and found that the rest of the world was dominated by Hitler and Mussolini. . . .*
>
> *And in the difficult hours of this day—through dark days that may be yet to come—we will know that the vast majority of the members of the human race are on our side.*

Source: "Fireside Chat: December 09, 1941." *American Presidency Project*, n.d., presidency.ucsb.edu. Accessed 19 Oct. 2023.

CHANGING MINDS

Imagine you are listening to this speech in 1941. Do you agree with Roosevelt's reasons for entering the war? Make sure you explain your opinion. Include facts and details to support your reasons.

IMPORTANT DATES

1922

Joseph Stalin becomes a leader of the Communist Party of the Soviet Union.

1925

Chiang Kai-shek becomes leader of the Chinese Nationalist Party.

1926

Hirohito becomes emperor of Japan.

1933

Franklin D. Roosevelt becomes president of the United States.

1934

Adolf Hitler takes the title of führer in Germany.

1940

Winston Churchill becomes British prime minister. Philippe Pétain orders France to surrender to Germany.

1943

Roosevelt, Churchill, and Stalin meet for the
Tehran Conference.

1945

Roosevelt dies and Harry S. Truman becomes president
of the United States. Hitler and Heinrich Himmler die by
suicide. Emperor Hirohito surrenders for Japan, and World
War II ends.

1946

Hermann Göring dies by suicide.

Tell the Tale

Chapter Two describes the key Allied and Axis leaders in Europe during World War II. Imagine you are living in one of the Allied countries during the war. What do you think of the country's leadership and strategies for the war? Do you support the leadership? Why or why not? Write 200 words about your experience.

Surprise Me

Chapter Three discusses the leadership of China and Japan during the war. After reading this chapter, what two or three facts about the topic did you find most surprising? Write a few sentences about each fact. Why did you find each fact surprising?

Take a Stand

In Chapter Four, you read the radio address President Roosevelt gave to the American people to prepare them for war. Do you agree that it was time for the United States to enter the war? Or do you think US leaders should have entered the war sooner?

Another View

Chapter Four discusses key leaders of the United States during World War II. As you know, every source is different. Ask an adult to help you find another source about US leaders during World War II. Write a short essay comparing the new source's views with those of this book's author. How are they similar and why? How are they different and why?

GLOSSARY

anti-Semitism
discrimination against
Jewish people

atomic bomb
an incredibly powerful
explosive weapon that uses
the energy released by
splitting atoms

charter
a written contract

communism
a system of government that
values common ownership
over private property

democracy
a government where people
have the power to elect
their leaders

drafted
selected for mandatory
military service

exiled
sent away from one's country
and not allowed to return

genocide
the large-scale destruction of
a particular group of people

nationalist
relating to the belief that one
nation is better than others
and other nations should
be more like it or should
not exist

occupy
to take over and control
another territory

ONLINE RESOURCES

To learn more about the leaders of World War II, visit our free resource websites below.

Visit **abdocorelibrary.com** or scan this QR code for free Common Core resources for teachers and students, including vetted activities, multimedia, and booklinks, for deeper subject comprehension.

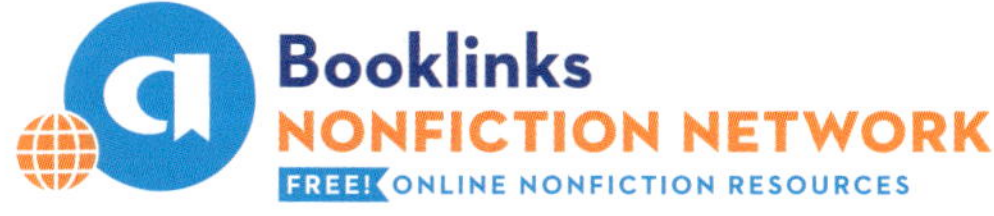

Visit **abdobooklinks.com** or scan this QR code for free additional online weblinks for further learning. These links are routinely monitored and updated to provide the most current information available.

LEARN MORE

Halls, Kelly Milner. *Heroes of World War II*. Rockridge, 2021.

Hudak, Heather C. *Causes of World War II*. Abdo, 2025.

Kanefield, Teri. *Franklin D. Roosevelt*. Abrams, 2019.

INDEX

About the Author

Yvette LaPierre lives in North Dakota with her family and advises students in the Indians Into Medicine Program at the University of North Dakota. She has written more than 30 books for children.